Tons of Trucks!

MAIL TRUCKS

By Martin Harasymiw

Gareth Stevens
PUBLISHING

Please visit our website, www.garethstevens.com. For a free color catalog of all our high-quality books, call toll free 1-800-542-2595 or fax 1-877-542-2596.

Library of Congress Cataloging-in-Publication Data
Names: Harasymiw, Martin, 1978- author.
Title: Mail trucks / Martin Harasymiw.
Description: New York : Gareth Stevens Publishing, [2022] | Series: Tons of trucks! | Includes index.
Identifiers: LCCN 2020025929 (print) | LCCN 2020025930 (ebook) | ISBN 9781538262870 (library binding) | ISBN 9781538262856 (paperback) | ISBN 9781538262863 (set) | ISBN 9781538262887 (ebook)
Subjects: LCSH: Postal service–United States–Juvenile literature. | Trucks–United States–Juvenile literature. | United States Postal Service–Juvenile literature.
Classification: LCC HE6371 .H38 2022 (print) | LCC HE6371 (ebook) | DDC 383/.1450284–dc23
LC record available at https://lccn.loc.gov/2020025929
LC ebook record available at https://lccn.loc.gov/2020025930

First Edition

Published in 2022 by
Gareth Stevens Publishing
111 East 14th Street, Suite 349
New York, NY 10003

Editor: Therese Shea
Designer: Deanna Paternostro

Photo credits: Cover, p. 1 Juan Camilo Bernal/Moment Mobile/Getty Images; p. 5 many wisteria/Shutterstock.com; p. 7 slobo/iStock/Getty Images Plus/Getty Images; pp. 9, 15 Karl_Sonnenberg/Shutterstock.com; p. 11 Joni Hanebutt/Shutterstock.com; pp. 13, 24 (mirror) PartArtGW/Shutterstock.com; p. 17 © iStock.com/THEPALMER; pp. 19, 24 (mailbox) Allkindza/iStock/Getty Images Plus/Getty Images; pp. 21, 23 Greg K__ca/Shutterstock.com.

Printed in the United States of America

Contents

This is my toy truck.
It's a mail truck!

This is a real mail truck.
It moves mail.

Mail trucks look small.
They carry a lot!
They move letters
and boxes.

PRIORITY MAIL
LABEL OTHER END
LABEL OTHER END

They have sliding doors.

UNITED STATES
POSTAL SERVICE

The truck has a
mirror in the back.
It helps the driver see.

mirror
Cochran
226582
www.usps.com
www.usps.com

The truck is filled
at the post office.

PRIORITY MAIL
ps.com

Drivers sit on
the right side.

www.usps.com
UNITED STATES
POSTAL SERVICE

They can
reach mailboxes!

Some mail trucks
are bigger.
They take mail
to far places.

UNITED STATES
POSTAL SERVICE

Mail trucks help!

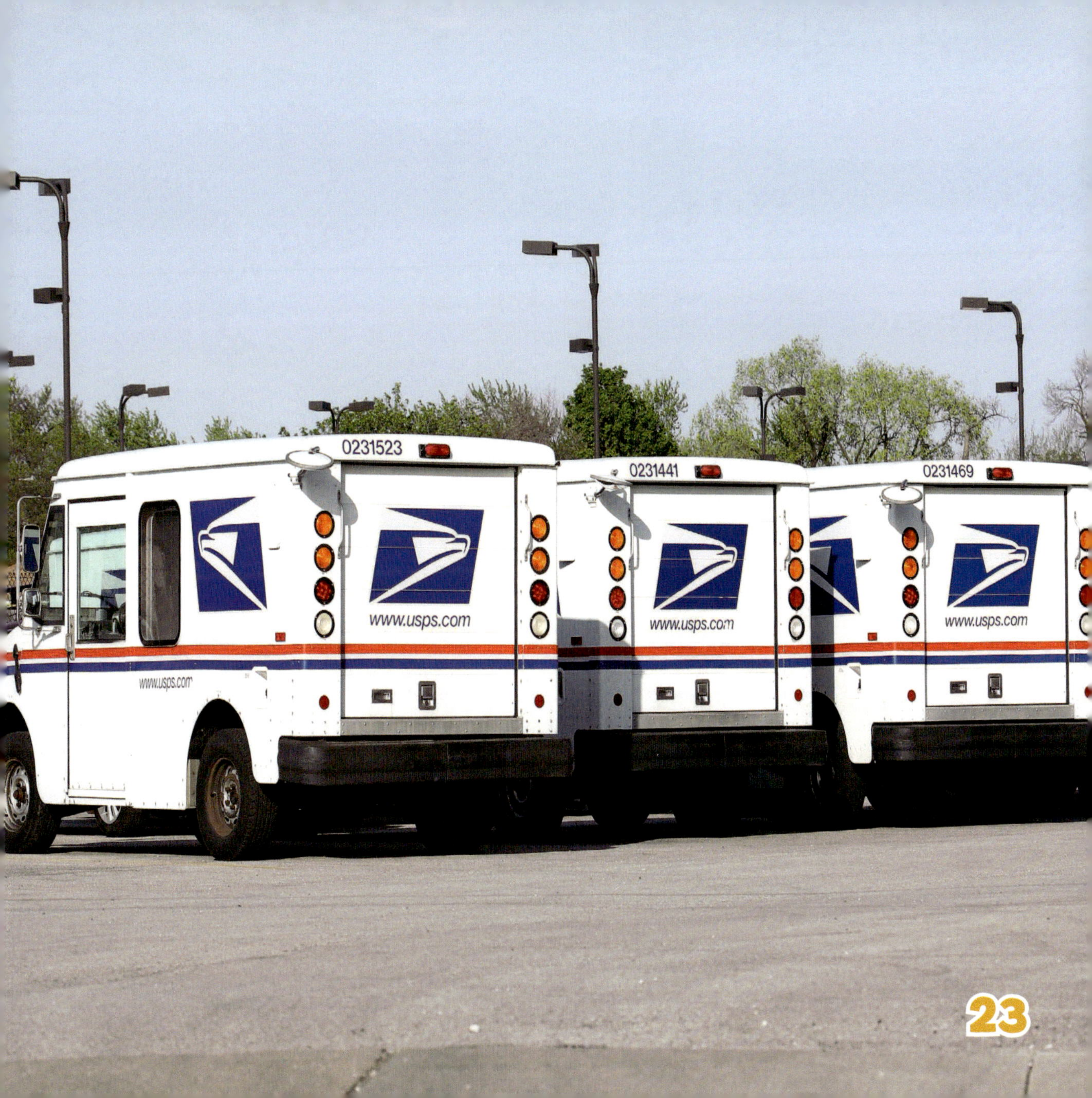
0231523
www.usps.com
www.usps.com
0231441
www.usps.com
0231469
www.usps.com

Words to Know

mailbox

mirror

Index